Sto Being Truthful With Yourself

By: Barb Bailey

Copyright Page

Published in the United States by Sanhedralite Editing and Publishing

ASIN: BOOKXDW7VY

ISBN: 978-1502578044

Edited by: Sherrie Arnoldy

Table of Contents

Copyright Page

Dedication

Forward

Why Continue To Suffer?

What Is The Importance In Being Truthful With Yourself?

How Do You Know You May Have Some Hidden Truths?

How Can You Become Truthful To Yourself?

What Are The Benefits To Being Truthful To Yourself?

Journaling

Meditational Practice

Simple Meditation Steps

My Positive Gift for You

Personal Journal Pages

Dedication

To Elizabest for being my personal truth
sounding board.

Forward

The beautiful concept of *The Blue Rainbow* series is to transform you from your blues to the lightness in life you deserve. I've created a safe environment where you can let go of what is holding you back. It is a very comfortable nook where you are gently guided and are encouraged to grow.

The *Blue Rainbow* series is a collection of purposely short guidance's and meditations. They have been created to convey single-focused topics.

The essence of this guidance is to help you grow, be truthful to yourself, and help you discover the freedom and happiness that is deep inside of you.

The subject of this book is powerfully practical. It was created based on questions and observations made by friends, family, and people I've mentored. The intention of this guidance is help you understand the significance of looking deep within. The corresponding free meditation is a gentle experience. It not only creates a safe environment, it allows you to be comfortable while connecting with yourself. The complimentary downloadable file can be found on my website www.barbbailey.com. Once there, you will find more information and be able to connect with so many other beautiful people like you.

The purpose of the meditation is to allow you to reconnect with yourself any time you feel the desire. Those of you who are new to meditation and experienced practitioners will all benefit from this guidance.

Why Continue To Suffer?

Do you feel yourself acting like a bitch, then feel terrible after? Part of you just wants to lash out, but you don't always understand why. Do you realize that these type of actions may be due to not being truthful with yourself? Do you realize that this isn't your true nature?

"The truth is a tsunami. We surf it or we die." Dr. David R Hawkins

This is not any easy subject. Being truthful to yourself is probably going to be one of the most difficult things you ever do. Once you accomplish this, the rewards are infinite!

If you are like most people, you have spent many years hiding away emotions from your past. You may have had no idea that they would surface again. In most cases, you aren't even aware that they are there; yet, you probably feel as though something is not right. There is the background nagging feeling in the pit of your stomach or a tightness in your chest or throat. In a sense, it is like a game you are playing. You know yourself the best; therefore, it's easiest to hide it from yourself. Once you do discover what these truths are, they will start to make complete sense. Feelings of relief will form as you begin to understand what is causing you unnecessary pain.

Positive unknown truths will have the tendency to arise as well. It is a misnomer that hidden behaviors are all unpleasant. Amazing, magical personal qualities can be uncovered as you look deep within.

By making it this far in this guidance, you are taking great steps forward for yourself. Truly appreciate yourself for being here!

Let me give you an example of why you should feel grateful. If you saw someone else become truthful with themselves would you look down upon them? Because they looked deep within and found some truth unknown to themselves, you would respect them for their courage and accomplishments. You can feel the same way about yourself.

Use this as encouragement to continue on progressing. You have been programmed a good part of your life to think and act certain ways. These behaviors have come from so many different directions. These sources most likely include, but are not limited to, parents, teachers, the media, well intended friends, celebrities, religious instructors, and other authority figures.

What Is The Importance In Being Truthful With Yourself?

The idea for this guidance initially started to flow out of me rapidly. I was excited to get the project rolling. I felt that although it is a difficult subject, I would be able to help many of you. Then I realized that I, too, needed to walk the walk myself.

I started to feel resistance when I sat down to write. I always physically write in my journal first, then type up the information later. It finally dawned on me as I was writing that I, too, was ready to face an inner truth that I was keeping from myself. The more I wrote in my journal, the more I uncovered a past repetitive relationship pattern in my life.

I was quite surprised when I discovered that the pattern stemmed from my parents separating. I had always remembered that I had felt relief. It had meant an end to all of the fighting and drama. I had always taken a false sense of pride that the divorce did not faze me. What I hadn't realized was that it impacted me in a different way than I had thought. I had a hard time admitting or even understanding what that impact was.

What I was not being truthful to myself about was the feeling of being forgotten. In my pre-teen life, I felt that I pretty much ceased to exist in my parents' lives. As an adult, I can easily look back and realize how mistaken I was. Unfortunately, I had carried this feeling with me throughout many of my relationships. I felt that my partner or sometimes friends, just plain old forgot I existed. In some cases I felt that I was only remembered when they needed something.

Until now, it has created unnecessary havoc and feelings of hurt in my life. Now, I can laugh at the absurdity of the situation and simultaneously feel compassion for myself. What a sense of freedom I have created by uncovering this distortion.

These types of self-imposed fallacies are creating emotional, physical, mental, and personal growth blockages in your life. These traits may consist of, but are not limited to, manipulation, addictions, self-doubt, dysfunctions, insecurities, and being untruthful to yourself and others.

The human mind is not capable of distinguishing truth from falsehood in other human beings. This is why it is so important that you take a deep look at yourself. You being honest creates a pathway for others to follow.

Once you are able to acknowledge the truths, the feeling of freedom can be immediate. Other times, the relief may be gradual. It depends on how your body rebalances itself. The self-honesty allows your heart to expand. This in turn gives you the gift of understanding others and sometimes intuit when others are not being truthful.

How Do You Know You May Have Some Hidden Truths?

1) Have you felt for a long time that something is not right, but you haven't been able to quite peg what it is? This may show up in the form of unsettling repetitive dreams.

2) You see patterns or behaviors in others that leave you feeling uneasy. Perhaps one of someone else's mannerisms really sinks its talons into your nerves.

3) You felt unexplained emotions towards others that didn't make sense because they really haven't done anything wrong. This can create feelings of self-doubt.

4) You have been in relationships where your partner has been untruthful to you. He or she has claimed that you were the same way to him or her. This truth at first can really cause a sinking feeling, which then gets transmuted into a sense of uplifting awareness.

How Can You Become Truthful To Yourself?

By being truthful to yourself first, it opens your ability to be truthful to others.

Once you become truthful with yourself, personal love and appreciation starts to take form. These feelings are not of a selfish nature. They are connecting you with your self and all of the amazing energy that is around you! You are opening yourself up for your true magic to shine through.

It can be scary the first time you look deep within yourself. Taking this first step allows the next step to come more easily.

You might be afraid you'll uncover what you consider to be embarrassing behaviors. These behaviors can cause you unnecessary feelings of shame or guilt. By acknowledging these traits, they lose their power. They no longer have control over you. You can decide what you want to do with them. You can keep them stuffed within or surrender them. Please visit my webpage www.barbbailey.com for more guidance's on how to let go of negative emotions.

Being truthful to yourself comes progressively. In very rare occurrences, new truths will reveal themselves to you without initial resistance. Your natural defense system does not expose you to more information than you can handle at a given time. Therefore, there is no need to be afraid that you will become overwhelmed. In other words the perfect information is presented to you at the perfect moment.

I have created a unique meditation that will help open yourself up in many different aspects. It will guide you through a gentle process of looking deep within. All you need to do is follow each step in the practice. If the meditation doesn't help you uncover any personal truths the first time, be patient and try it again. It could be that your subconscious is not yet ready to reveal something new to you. Respect yourself for the initial attempt, then embrace the experience again soon.

There will most likely be moments of resistance as the old ways want to hang on. Accept that the resistance is there, then continue on the process of being truthful to yourself. Do not get discouraged if you don't get immediate apparent results. A lot is happening in the background of self-awareness. Keep working on uncovering the behaviors that are no longer welcomed in your life.

Have compassion for yourself throughout the entire process. You are taking huge steps towards personal growth and transformation!

Respect and take joy in the new courage you have found.

What Are The Benefits To Being Truthful To Yourself?

By acknowledging these truths, you are starting to let go of the control they have over you. They have been holding back true happiness that is innately yours. You have the ability to transform negative energy into positive energy simply by being straightforward with yourself.

Being truthful to yourself helps you build your self-confidence. It creates a better understanding that you are beautiful regardless of what has shaped your life.

Uncovering the true you allows yourself to shine forward. This releases you from any emotional burdens that you have unintentionally created for yourself. These burdens can cause you to lose clarity of thought, thus causing everyday life to become more difficult. When you start to think and feel clearer you are giving your destiny room to manifest.

Remember that you have positive truths to discover as well. The rewards of uncovering this beautiful inner you are limitless.

How you feel on the inside emanates outward. This feeling of freedom is contagious to those who are around you; in kind, giving them the courage to be truthful with themselves.

Journaling

I'm a big advocate of journaling. I write at least daily in my journaling. I find it is easiest to put, at a minimum, an outline of a project down prior to starting. It allows me to stay centered and gives me something to refer back to. Most importantly, it allows me to connect with my inner self. The more you journal the more you will understand what your inner self is.

Are you one who likes to organize your thoughts before starting a project? Most people find that they can clear their minds and bring out their creativity by writing them down first.

When you simply writing down your intentions or ideas, it allows for a more relaxed, focused process. Your journaling can be as vague or detailed as you wish. In many cases, your journal can be used as a form of confession. It is a private nook where you can get things off of your chest. Many studies have been conducted showing the value of documenting your emotional experiences.

Journaling is a fantastic way to start to uncover the truths you have been hiding from yourself. Follow the corresponding guided meditation, then document what you have learned. More than likely it will enhance your ability to contemplate deeper thoughts. Writing is also an excellent way to clear your mind before going to sleep. Jot down what is bothering you before you close your eyes for the night. This tables the topic so that it doesn't keep you awake.

I keep a pen and paper next to bed to record ideas and dreams that may appear in the night. That way these glimpses of magic do not dissolve come morning.

I find it is easiest if you have a designated book or pad of paper. I've created specific personal journals for this purpose. They correspond with *The Blue Rainbow* series, website, and meditation energies. You can purchase the paperback version *The Blue Rainbow Series Journals* on Amazon. More details for these journals and other personal growth experiences can be found in my other guidance's and website.

If you are new to journaling, I suggest you sit down with your book at least once a day. Grab a favorite pen and find a comfortable place to sit. This journal is all about you. Here is the place you can write anything you like. Draw pictures if you choose. If you are not sure how to start, write the date and any thoughts or emotions that surface. The beauty of it is that whatever you write is the perfect thing for the moment.

Use your journaling time to discover, laugh, cry, and be with yourself.

Meditational Practice

Meditation is scientifically proven to alleviate stress, anxiety, and depression.

Every time you meditate, think of it as your time to take a break from everyday life. Preferably it is a daily practice where you can set all worries and endless thoughts aside. Allow yourself the time for these few precious moments.

Meditation allows your body, mind, and soul to take a break from the everyday stressors of life. The sound of your breath as you breathe deeply has a natural calming quality to it. Meditation grants you the ability to open you heart and become more aware of your surroundings. As your awareness increases, so does your wisdom and inner tranquility.

I've had several people tell me they don't practice meditation. They confessed they simply don't know how and were afraid to ask. They felt everyone knew how to meditate but them. Think of the word meditation as a generic term. In the case of this guidance it does not have strict parameters.

I have created a gently guided *How To be Truthful with Yourself* Meditation to get you started. This downloadable file will guide you every step of the way. You will benefit regardless if you are new to meditation or are an experienced practitioner.

Simple Meditation Steps

Wear loose clothing that will not inhibit you to relax or breathe deeply and comfortably. If possible, retreat to a space where the meditation is the sole focus. Turn off any other distracting sounds like a TV, radio, message notifications or any other noise that may distract you. You can always follow up with the rest of your life when you finish.

Start by getting in a comfortable, relaxed position that will allow you to focus for fifteen to twenty minutes. This position can be lying down or sitting in a chair. To be effective, you do not need to be sitting in the standard meditation cross legged position.

Follow each step of the gently guided corresponding audio meditation. It may seem a bit awkward to you at first. Follow each of the breathing practices that are taught in the meditation. The ability to slow your breathing down comes with ease and grace over time.

It is very common to lose your focus when you first learn how to meditate. This is especially true as you first start to uncover personal truths. Your mind will most likely start to wander. When you notice this starting to happen, redirect your awareness back to the audio file.

It is common in meditations to have key phrases repeated throughout the practice. In some cases, the same meaning will be said using different words. This allows you to benefit even more from the focused topic.

Occasionally, you may feel worse after meditating. This is because emotions are coming to the surface. There is no need to judge these emotions. Allow them to flow. It is a deeper part of you wanting to let go of stored negative emotions. It is your personal magic telling you that they are no longer welcomed. These emotions can be documented in your journal for better self-understanding. By practicing daily, the benefits of meditating will greatly increase for you.

My Positive Gift for You

Congratulations for coming this far and taking a deeper look at how to stop being a bitch by becoming truthful with yourself. Reading this book and following the corresponding meditation allows the energy to flow for continuous positive transformation.

The corresponding meditation has been created specifically to guide you into a deeper connection with yourself. It will gently give you the tools on how to make powerful upgrades to your current life. The meditation directs you through several breathing steps that allow for clarity while maintaining a feeling of safeness. I really encourage you to practice it multiple times, especially when difficult behaviors begin to surface. The more you participate in the meditation, the easier it will be to send these behaviors packing.

Please visit me on my website and corresponding private Facebook page. While visiting you can join many others who, too, are on their path for personal growth and transformation. Read the colorful stories of others who have been inspired to share their experiences. It's a wonderful place for you to document your uplifting experiences and share your personal stories.

When it comes to negative emotions, is there a particular subject you would like to learn about or would like more clarity? Reach out and contact me. I would love to hear from you. Not only am I available for personal mentoring, I'm very excited to create more books, training, and meditations. Ask me how I can help you get out of your rut and back into your groove.

Always remember that - positive energy is searching for you as much as you are searching for it.

I'm really looking forward to connecting with you again soon.

Many smiles,

Barb

P.S. Thank you for experiencing this guidance and meditation on how to *Stop Being a Bitch by Being Truthful with Yourself.* If you have benefited from this experience and found it useful, kindly write a short review. Your support really does make a difference, and I read all the reviews personally.

Thanks again for your support!

Here are a few more books from *The Blue Rainbow Series* which you will benefit:

Remote Energy: How to Healing Energy to Someone you love

How to Heal Your Wounded Heart so You Can Love Freely

Resentment: How to Let Go of Bitterness in an Entertaining Way

How to Write Off Guilt: Setting Free the Past through Journaling

How to Detach from Negative People

Serving up Shame: Freedom from the Emotions that Originate from Alcoholic Parents

Only Those Who Dare Truly Awaken: A Guidebook to Discovering Your Personal Magic

Strolling Thru the Crossroads of Self-Doubt: A Unique Guide in Discovering Clear Personal Direction

An Uplifting Journey in Discovering Personal Healing: Cleansing Rain Renewal Guide and Meditation

The Blue Rainbow Series Personal Journals (available in paperback on Amazon)

My Truthful Journey starts here:

_____

_____

_____

_____

_____

_____

_____

_____

_____

_____

_____

_____

_____

_____

_____

By becoming truthful with myself, I have personally gifted myself the freedom to live the life I truly deserve.

CPSIA information can be obtained
at www.ICGtesting.com
Printed in the USA
LVHW031558080520
655240LV00004B/1451

CPSIA information can be obtained
at www.ICGtesting.com
Printed in the USA
LVHW031558080520
655240LV00004B/1451

9 781502 578044